Umbria Travel Guide

Sightseeing, Hotel, Restaurant & Shopping Highlights

James Crawford

Copyright © 2014, Astute Press
All Rights Reserved.

No part of this publication may be reproduced, stored in a retrieval system, or transmitted, in any form or by any means without the prior written permission of the publisher, nor be otherwise circulated in any form of binding or cover other than that in which it is published and without similar condition being imposed on the subsequent purchaser.

If there are any errors or omissions in copyright acknowledgements the publisher will be pleased to insert the appropriate acknowledgement in any subsequent printing of this publication.

Although we have taken all reasonable care in researching this book we make no warranty about the accuracy or completeness of its content and disclaim all liability arising from its use

Table of Contents

Umbria **6**
    Culture 8
    Location & Orientation 9
    Climate & When to Visit 10
Sightseeing Highlights **11**
    Perugia **11**
        San Lorenzo Cathedral 13
        Maggiore Fountain 14
        Palazzo dei Priori 14
        Galleria Nazionale dell'Umbria 15
        Rocca Paolina 15
    Gubbio **16**
        Palazzo dei Consoli 17
        Museo Civico 17
        Cathedral 18
        Palazzo Ducale 18
        Teatro Romano 19
    Assisi **19**
        Basilica Santa Maria degli Angeli 20
        Basilica di San Francesco 21
        Tempio di Minerva 22
        Rocca Maggiore 23
        Eremo delle Carceri 23
    Spoleto **24**
        Duomo 25
        Ponte delle Torri 25
        Casa Romana 26
    Todi **26**
        Santa Maria della Consolazione 27
        Piazza del Popolo 27
        Todi Cathedral 28
        Tempio di San Fortunato 28
    Orvieto **29**
        Orvieto Cathedral 29
    Lake Trasimeno **30**
        Castiglione del Lago 30

  Panicale 31
  Isla Polvese 31
  Isla Maggiore 31
  Vernazzano 32
  Tuoro 32

Recommendations for the Budget Traveller 33
Places To Stay 33
  Hotel Sacro Cuore 33
  P&P Assisi Camere 34
  Hotel Roma 35
  Agriturismo Casale dei Frontini 35
  Hotel Trasimeno 36
Places To Eat & Drink 37
  Ristorante Pizzeria Capri 37
  Osteria Piazzetta dell'Erba 37
  Osteria del Trivio 38
  Il Giglio d'Oro 38
  DivinPeccato 39
Places To Shop 39
  Mercato Mensile Antiquariato 39
  Augusta Perusia Cioccolate e Gelateria 40
  Leo Grilli Arte 40
  Terra Umbra 41
  Bartolomei Orvieto 41

Umbria

Umbria is located in Italy's green centre between Tuscany, La Marche and Lazio. This small, landlocked region has less than a million inhabitants but is proud of its historic cities including Perugia, Orvieto and Assisi. Umbria offers idyllic ancient towns perched on scenic hills, each one with a rich artistic and architectural heritage.

Umbria's name hails from the tribe Umbrii – possibly the oldest one in Italy – that controlled the land which is now Umbria as well as parts of today's Tuscany and La Marche. The Umbrii influence is mostly felt in the eastern part of the region, while the western part (including Perugia and Orvieto) has an Etruscan-inspired history, hence the more somber atmosphere.

The Middle Ages in Italy were marked by bloody battles between the independent city states, causing the Umbrians to retreat into the fortified towns. But after many years of warfare, the region stagnated over a period of multiple centuries only to be rediscovered recently. Foreign purchases of local rural property have increased significantly - much like they did in Tuscany a few decades ago - but the identity and cultural tradition of Umbria remains untouched.

Perhaps the most known fact about Umbria is linked to the city of Assisi as this small town is the birthplace of the well-known St. Francis of Assisi. This spiritual influence has often resulted in Umbria being referred to as the 'land of saints', perfectly complimented by the mystical landscape and the peculiar Umbrian light.

Most visitors start their Umbrian adventure in the capital Perugia and almost all make a stop in Assisi. But there is so much more than these two towns waiting to be discovered in Umbria; majestic sights include the grand Gothic Duomo (Cathedral) in Orvieto, the perfectly medieval town of Gubbio, the quintessential Umbrian Spoleto and Italy's largest Lake – Lago Trasimeno. Each of these towns is likely to keep you busy and entertained for at least a day and traveling between them is quite straightforward.

There is a something for everyone in Umbria; be it the student-fueled nightlife in Perugia or the fairy-tale atmosphere of the small town Todi, the region is bound to capture your heart with its history, tradition and lifestyle and have you wonder why you haven't visited earlier.

Culture

Umbria's culture is a definitely influenced by its history spanning three millennia and heavily doused with mysticism and spirituality. This land of saints is not only home to the well-known St. Francis of Assisi but also to St. Valentine and St. Benedict. In every town around Umbria one can find a grandiose cathedral and inside each are precious artistic treasures made by masters such as Giotto, Raphael and Lorenzetti.

But nowadays, Umbria is not only spiritual and historic – it is also modern and delightful. Popular annual events such as the Umbria Jazz and the Eurochocolate festival in Perugia each October provide a welcome break from the overload of cathedral, churches and palaces.

Umbria is decidedly apt at maintaining traditions and heritages. Don't be surprised by unlocked front doors, grandmothers making pasta by hand and a general devotion to an exquisite cuisine mostly revolving around truffles, cheese and olives. Remarkable red and white wines from Umbria are also becoming widely requested around the world.

Location & Orientation

The majority of travelers arriving to Umbria by air land in Rome, a three hour drive away. Perugia has its own airport which is quite small but does have flights arriving from Milan, London and Barcelona, some of which are organized by low-cost airlines. Other budget options are the airports of Pisa and Bologna, frequently served by low-cost carriers.

Between them, the Umbrian towns are all connected by bus (umbriamobilita.it) though train lines (trenitalia.com) may be the smarter choice for some routes. Do research the location of the train station in the town you want to travel to as they are often quite remote from the city centers (particularly in Orvieto, Todi, Perugia and Assisi). Gubbio is only accessible via bus. Note that both train and bus tickets need stamping after purchase (at the machines on platforms or on board).

Those choosing to drive around Umbria will likely arrive to Perugia via the A1 autostrada running from Rome to Milan. There are advantages to driving around the region as it will give you the option to explore more remote rural sections. However, try to use the vehicle as a means of getting from one town to the other only and not for navigation within the towns themselves; most historic centers provide limitations on driving and parking.

Climate & When to Visit

Every season seems to be charming in Umbria, with the spring offering the best color show as wildflowers overtake the landscape. For extraordinary countryside views, visit Umbria in May. Though summers are marked by the attractive yellow sunflowers along the lush valleys, July and August are generally hot with averages of 28 °C (82 °F) and quite crowded. Winters are cold and dry with average lows around 2 °C (36 °F) but for those preferring the off-season, they do provide the advantage of a dense indoor cultural agenda around the many galleries and museums.

Perhaps the best season to have it all is early fall; September and October see less rainfall than the spring months and the crowds are mostly gone.

Sightseeing Highlights

Perugia

The affluent provincial capital of Perugia is the most likely starting point on any Umbria exploring trail. A remarkably preserved hill town where the past meets the present, it is a vibrant student center with two universities and over 30,000 students.

Architecturally mostly intact in the last 4 centuries, most of Perugia revolves around a single street; the famous Corso Vannucci named after the city's best-known artist Pietro Vannucci (Perugino). This promenade is a true people-watching heaven, well seasoned with cafes and restaurants.

The cultural agenda in Perugia is rich, with many art events, concerts and performances scheduled year-round as well as a heavy sprinkling of museums and churches. Events like the Umbria Jazz, one of the most acclaimed regional music events, as well ast he annual Eurochocolate – the international chocolate festival – are certainly two events worth planning your trip around.

Intercity buses connect Perugia's Piazza Partigiani with many other towns in the region including Assisi, Todi, Gubbio and Lago Trasimeno. For up to date information on bus routes, visit the APM Perugia website (www.apmperugia.com). Taking a train may be a better option if you are headed to Spello, Spoleto or Orvieto, and trains leave from the Perugia train station on Piazza Vittorio Veneto. Trains also connect Perugia to Rome, Florence and Arezzo.

A difficult city to navigate by car, most of Perugia's city center is open only for commercial traffic and can't be accessed unless you have a confirmed hotel booking. Bus rides cost €1 and go as far as Piazza Italia in the historic center. A MiniMetro (small driverless train) is also a good option to go from the main station to the center of the town. Visitors may also opt to rent a scooter (about €20/day) for a more independent travel.

San Lorenzo Cathedral

Piazza 4 Novembre, 6, 06123 Perugia
Tel: +39 075 572 3832
http://www.diocesi.perugia.it/

The most famous orientation point in Perugia is the Cathedral of San Lorenzo (also known as Perugia Cathedral) - a Middle Age Cathedral started in 1345 and heavily added upon in the 15th and 16th centuries. A Fra Bevignate project built over ancient basilica ruins, its exterior is decorated in white and pink marble and was never fully completed.

The Cathedral is also the famed home of Virgin Mary's wedding ring stolen in 1488 which is nowadays kept in the Holy Ring Chapel on the left, equipped with 15 locks. Twice a year – on July 30th and the second to last Sunday in January – it is displayed to the public. When in the Cathedral, marvel at the Madonna of Grace to the right of the entrance, done by Giannicola di Paolo. The interior is a Gothic drama masterpiece; take a peek at the San Bernardino Chapel with Barocci's Deposition. The Cathedral is open Monday through Saturday from 07:30 to 12:30 and from 16:00 to 18:00. On Sundays, its working hours are 08:00-12:00 and 16:00-18:30. It is accessible through the municipal bus transportation system as most buses stop on the nearby Piazza Italia.

Maggiore Fountain

Piazza 4 Novembre, 06123 Perugia

Just outside the Cathedral is the magnificent 1278-built Fontana Maggiore (Great Fountain), done by sculptors Nicola and Giovanni Pisano. Embellished with figures of the zodiac and artistic symbols, the fountain also features bas relief scenes from the Old Testament as well as a griffin – Perugia's city symbol. Like the Cathedral, it was designed by Fra Bevignate and part of the civic improvement program aimed at celebrating the free Perugia commune.

Palazzo dei Priori

Corso Vannucci 19, 06121 Perugia
Tel: +39 075 586 68410

One of Italy's best known public palaces, the Palazzo dei Priori is located just across the Perugia Cathedral and on the corner of the main street Corso Vannucci. Built in an Italian Gothic style of the early 14th century, it was the seat of the priori (first class citizens) and nowadays hosts the Town Hall. The portal on the main Piazza is marked by the city's symbols – the griffin and the lion. The keys to the gates of Siena are also strung above the door, marking Perugia's victory at the battle of Torrita in 1358.

Galleria Nazionale dell'Umbria

Corso Vannucci 19, 06121 Perugia
Tel: +39 075 586 68410
www.gallerianazionaleumbria.it

On the fourth floor of the gothic Palazzo dei Priori, Umbria's largest and most refined art gallery can be found. The Galleria Nazionale dell'Umbria hosts a collection of works done by local and regional artists such as Pintoricchio, Perugino, Gentile da Fabriano and Duccio displayed in its 30 gallery rooms. Besides paintings, visitors can also admire frescoes and sculptures while a section dedicated to the evolution of the city of Perugia is also part of the Gallery. Strongly recommended for all Renaissance art lovers, the Gallery is open from 08:30 to 19:30 daily except on Mondays. Entrance costs €8; €4 for EU citizens 18-25 years of age.

Rocca Paolina

Piazza Italia, 06122 Perugia
Tel: +39 075 572 8440

For a dose of labyrinth-like exploration and a shelter from the summer heat, head to the Rocca Paolina – Perugia's atmospheric underground city. Initially an integral section of the Palazzo della Provincia fortress built between 1540 and 1543.

It was partially destroyed after the end of Pope Paul III's rule, but what is left can be visited by taking the escalators from Piazza Italia which move through the underground ruins and down to Via Masi. The various empty spaces in the Rocca Paolina are often venues for exhibits and host the monthly antiques market (last weekend of each month). The cost for the escalator ride is €3.50. Besides the main entrance from Piazza Italia, Rocca Paolina can also be accessed through Via Marzia, Via Masi and Viale Indipendenza.

Gubbio

As an interesting half-day or full-day trip from the capital Perugia, take the bus or drive north to medieval Gubbio, an imposing town perched on the steep and green slopes of the Monte Ingino. Its nickname – City of Silence – perfectly captures its quiet atmosphere which is attractively embellished by the colourful setting of the town. In the 14th century, Gubbio belonged to the Montefeltro family of Urbino, only to be subsequently incorporated in the Papal States. Nowadays, it stands somewhat isolated from Umbria (and neighboring Tuscany and La Marche), therefore making it a less likely tourist magnet.

Walking is definitely the best way to explore Gubbio's picturesque streets and most of its sights are within a ten minute uphill walk from the central bus station. You may be interested in taking the funicular ride to the top of Monte Ingino but be warned that it is not for those suffering from fear of heights.

Palazzo dei Consoli

Piazza Grande, 06024 Gubbio
Tel: +39 075 927 4298

The medieval Palazzo dei Consoli built between 1332 and 1337 overtakes the attention of those arriving at the Piazza Grande and dominates the town. A local architect by the name of Gattapone is sometimes credited for this striking palace which used to be the home of the Parliament of Gubbio. Today housing the town hall and the Civic Museum, the Palazzo's terrace provides spectacular views over Gubbio. Those arriving at the Piazza Quaranta Martiri at the bottom of Gubbio can use the elevators to ride up to the Palace.

Museo Civico

Piazza Grande, Palazzo dei Consoli, 06024 Gubbio
Tel: +39 075 927 4298

Housed in the Palazzo dei Consoli, the Civic Museum displays the famous Eugubine Tablets – seven bronze tablets discovered in 1444 and providing insight into the ancient and obscure dead language of Umbria using Etruscan and Latin characters. A gallery with works of Gubbian artists can also be found in the museum. Entrance costs €5 and the Museum is open daily from 10:00 to 13:00 and from 15:00 to 18:00 (14:00 to 17:00 in the winter).

Cathedral

Via Federico da Montefeltro, 06024 Gubbio

A short walk up the central Via Ducale, Gubbio's Duomo dedicated to the Saints Marian and James dates from the late 12th century and features a distinctly pink façade and a 12th century stained glass window. Symbols of the Evangelists (eagle, lion, angel and ox) can be observed on the sides. A fresco most likely done by Pinturicchio is located inside as well as a precious wooden Christ over the altar, exhibiting a clear influence of the Umbrian school. The Cathedral is open from 08:00 to 12:30 and from 15:00 to 19:00 daily. For those visiting it right after the Palazzo dei Consoli, a second elevator connects the two sights.

Palazzo Ducale

Via Ducale, 06024 Gubbio
Tel: +39 075 927 5872

Just across from the Duomo, the Palazzo Ducale - dating from the 15th century (1470) - was built by Montefeltro family as a smaller scale duplicate of their Urbino Palace. A lovely Renaissance-inspired courtyard can be found inside the walls as well as a small museum. Entrance to the Palace costs €5 and it can be visited from 09:00 to 19:30 every day except Monday.

Teatro Romano

Viale Teatro Romano, 06024 Gubbio

Just off Viale Teatro Romano, the Roman Theatre complex is what remains of the 1st century theatre, nowadays often hosting outdoor concerts and lectures in the summer. Square blocks of native limestone can be seen in this site where the original diameter of the cave was about 70 meters. The Teatro Romano is open from 08:30 to 19:30 (13:30 in the winter). Objects found during the excavations are displayed in the nearby Antiquarium.

Assisi

Back in Perugia from Gubbio, the next stop on your Umbria trail is likely the region's spiritual center Assisi, some 25 kilometers to the southeast and reachable by bus, train or car. Most notably known as the home of St. Francis, this beautiful town is one of the most important pilgrimage sites in the world. Originally an Umbri settlement in the 7th century BC and conquered around the 3rd century BC, Assisi was Christianized by Saint Rufino but was put on the map because of St. Francis – the patron saint of Italy whose heritage lives on in Assisi's streets. It was here, in his hometown, that St. Francis had his visions and calls from God after spending his formative years largely removed from religious life. He began to preach and beg, renounced his sizable inheritance and later founded the Franciscan order.

Be prepared to face crowds during the day as Assisi is famous with tourists and pilgrims alike. The city does calm down toward the evening when day-trippers leave and it regains its small-town charm.

Basilica Santa Maria degli Angeli

Piazza Porziuncola, 1, 06081 Assisi
Tel: +39 075 805 1430
http://www.porziuncola.org/home/

Before you enter the town of Assisi in the Tiber valley, you are greeted by the 16th century Basilica di Santa Maria degli Angeli. The Basilica was designed in the Mannerst style and encloses the tiny but sacred Porziuncola Chapel - St.Francis' first refuge and the site where he renounced the world and started the Franciscan movement.

Nowadays, the Basilica is the seventh largest Christian church and features a dome with eight windows and cornices directly under which the Porziuncola is situated. In 1684, a bell tower was added to the church but the whole structure was severely impacted by the 1832 earthquake and later reconstructed. Make sure you get a good look of the gold statue of Madona degli Angeli done by Colasanti and added on top of the façade in 1930.

Inside, decorations are scarce with the exception of the side chapels which include works done by Circignani, Appiani and Salimbeni. A wooden choir carved by the Franciscans as well as the altar and the cathedral are its main features. The Chapel of Transito is the location of St. Francis' death, just against the right columns of the dome.

The Basilica is open from 06:15 to 12:30 and from 14:30 to 19:30. Santa Maria degli Angeli is located at the foot of the Assisi hill, close to the train station.

Basilica di San Francesco

Piazza San Francesco, 2, 06081 Assisi
Tel: +39 075 819 001
www.sanfrancescoassisi.org

Assisi's past soaked in St. Francis' influence can be observed in the two churches dedicated to the saint - a Romanesque lower one and a Gothic upper one – jointly a UNESCO World Heritage Site. The construction of the lower one started shortly after St. Francis' death and his coffin can be found in a crypt just under the lower Basilica which is a dim and somber venue illuminated by candles.

Decorations in the Lower Church's chapels include work done by Simone Martini from Siena, Cimabue and possibly by Giotto. Here you can also see some of the most famous works of Pietro Lorenzetti, the master from Siena, such as Madonna with Sts. John and Francis and the powerful Crucifixion. Also worth noting is the fresco of St. Clare. To see relics of St. Francis, check out the Treasury (Tesoro) up the steps next to the altar. The Lower church is open daily from 06:00 to 18:45. Photography is not allowed and silence is required.

The upper Basilica, by contrast, is quite bright and features frescoes by young Giotto, arranged in a sequence. Perhaps the most famous one is St. Francis Preaching to the Birds which has been frequently reproduced worldwide. The Upper Church is open daily from 08:30 to 18:45. Do note that appropriate dress is required in the Basilicas; admission is free.

Tempio di Minerva

Piazza del Comune, 06081 Assisi
Tel: +39 075 812 361

Facing the Piazza del Comune, the Tempio di Minerva (Minerva's Temple) dates from the Roman times during Emperor Augustus when it was a pagan temple dedicated to Minerva – the goddess of wisdom. Nowadays a church dedicated to Mary, it was previously also used as a monastery and prison. The exterior of the temple is classical but the interior is largely baroque due to the multiple transformations, mostly done in the 17th century. The Roman façade is still mostly intact as are the six Corinthian columns.

Admission to the Minerva Temple is free and its opening hours are 07:30 – 12:00 and 14:00 to 19:00 Monday through Saturday. On Sundays the temple opens one hour later.

Rocca Maggiore

Piazzale delle Libertà Comunali, 06081 Assisi
Tel: +39 075 815 5234

The 14th century Rocca Maggiore is the hill fortress with spectacular views, impressively dominating Assisi. Earliest evidence of its existence dates back to 1174, when it was a German feudal castle. Rebuilt in 1367 by Cardinal Albornoz, a twelve-sided tower was added to it in 1458 as was the wall connecting the castle to the city. Head up the winding passageways for impressive photo ops at sunset and spectacular views of the Spoleto valley. Travelers can wander around the Rocca Maggiore Tuesday through Sunday from 10:00 to sunset. Entrance costs €5.

Eremo delle Carceri

Eremo delle Carceri, 06081 Assisi
Tel: +39 075 812 301
www.eremocarceri.it

A set of caves right above Assisi in the protected forest of Monte Subasio, the Eremo delle Carceri (Hermitage of Prisons) was St. Frencis' chosen retirement location where he could devote himself to prayer. A number of religious buildings can be found on the site which remains quite peaceful and is still the home of a number of Franciscan monks.

The Eremo delle Carceri is some 4 kilometers east of Assisi's center, and is a prime spot for hiking and picnicking offering a truly tranquil environment with views across Umbria. The Hermitage is open daily from 06:30 to 18:00 (19:00 in the summer). Admission is free but donations are encouraged.

Spoleto

Some 50 kilometers south of Assisi, Spoleto is a charming walled city situated on a hillside. With its two kilometers of walls and a historic importance dating from the time when the Lombards made it a capital, Spoleto was once powerful enough to aim for the throne and was, though very briefly, even the Empire's capital.

Most of Spoleto's sights can be found towards the top of the hill and this upper part of the old town is connected to the train and bus stations by a shuttle service. The quaint town has become popular due to the Festival of Two Worlds – a summer festival combining theatre, music, dance and poetry which revived the city in the middle of the 20th century, after a long period of decline.

Duomo

Piazza del Duomo, 2, Spoleto
Tel: +39 074 344 307

Perhaps one of the most refined cathedrals in Umbria, the 12th century Romanesque Duomo dedicated to the Assumption of Mary is attractively marked by eight rose windows. Original floor tiles inside date to a previous church destroyed in the 12th century. A remodeling performed in the 17th century added notable Renaissance touches to the Cathedral, including the porch.

Just above the entrance one can see Bernini's bust of Pope Urban VIII while frescoes painted by Fra Filippo Lippi in the 15th century can also be found inside and include the Annunciation, Nativity and Dormition. Look up to the magnificent Coronation of the Virgin decorating the half dome. Lippi died before completing his work on the Cathedral and his tomb is located in the right transept. Pinturicchio's work also adorns the Cappella Eroli. The Cathedral is open daily from 08:00 to 12:30 and from 15:00 to 17:30 (19:00 in the summer). Entrance is free.

Ponte delle Torri

The Bridge of Towers (Ponte delle Torri) was built in the 14th century and is one of Umbria's most famous monuments. Spanning the ravine between Spoleto and the mountain, the bridge is 80 meters high and 230 meters long and features a set of ten Gothic arches.

Underneath it, a Roman aqueduct used to exist while its elevation provides exquisite views of the valley from the balcony in the center.

Casa Romana

Via di Visiale, Spoleto
Tel: + 39 074 323 4350

Remains from Roman times have been excavated around Spoleto and traced back to the 1st century. Perhaps the most remarkably preserved one is the Casa Romana (Roman House) east of Piazza della Liberta and under the Palazzo Comunale. The house belonged to the mother of Emperor Vespasian and provides insight into what a typical Roman period house looked like. A large atrium around which rooms are arranged was built on top of a rain cistern. Rooms feature delightful monochromatic geometric mosaics.

Todi

Smaller than Spoleto but perfectly quintessential as an Italian hill town, Todi is located some 50 kilometers to the northwest and is excellently positioned in the center of the region thus well suited to act as a base from which to explore Umbria. The walls encircling this town of 17,000 tell story upon story; from Etruscan and Umbrian hints in the interior walls to the Roman middle walls and all the way out to the Middle Ages' external walls. In recent years, the town has become a magnet for foreign expats, intellectuals and artists.

Santa Maria della Consolazione

Viale della Consolazione, 06059 Todi
Tel: + 39 074 323 4350

Todi's most famous church, the Renaissance Chiesa di Santa Maria della Consolazione, is an exquisite architectural work with perfect geometry. Found just outside the city walls, its soaring dome can be seen from quite afar. Its construction was started in 1508 and was completed in 1607 with a myriad of architects involved in its evolving design. An image of the Madonna, discovered during the construction and believed to be miraculous, is housed in the altar. The church is open daily from 09:30 to 12:00 and from 14:30 to 18:30 (17:00 in the winter).

Piazza del Popolo

Piazza del Popolo, 06059 Todi

The famed Piazza del Popolo is the perfect postcard image of Todi and one of the best known Italian squares. With a medieval cathedral and numerous historic buildings, its internal section used to be enclosed within four gates during the medieval period. Built on top of Roman cisterns, the Piazza del Popolo is nowadays the perfect place for enjoying a cup of coffee.

Todi Cathedral

Piazza del Popolo, 06059 Todi
Tel: +39 075 894 3041

The northwestern end of the Piazza is reserved for the Cathedral – a 12th century Gothic work of art with a spectacular 16th century rose window decorated with cherubs. The current church was actually rebuilt after a fire burned down the previous structure in 1190. The façade is simple but the woodwork on the interior is extremely intricate. Check out the enormous fresco of the Universal Judgement by Faenzone with a clear Michelangelo influence. The Todi Cathedral is open from 08:30 to 12:30 and from 14:30 to 18:30.

Tempio di San Fortunato

Piazza Umberto 1, 06059 Todi

The Tempio di San Fortunato - begun in 1292 and never fully completed - is the home of frescoes done by Masolino da Panicale and houses the tomb of Beato Jacapone, Todi's patron saint. For breathtaking views of Todi's surroundings, climb up to the Campanile di San Fortunato. The Tempio is open from 10:00 to 19:00 (17:00 in the winter); closed between 13:00 and 14:30 and all day on Tuesdays.

Orvieto

About 40 kilometers southwest of Todi, Orvieto balances on a cliff made of volcanic ash stone. Originally founded by the Etruscans, Orvieto is nowadays popular and crowded in the summertime mostly due to its location on the main road from Rome to Florence, making it an Umbrian pit stop even for those headed elsewhere.

Orvieto Cathedral

Plaza Duomo, Orvieto

A truly breathtaking sight even from far away, the Orvieto Cathedral was started in 1290 most likely by Fra Bevignate and is perhaps one of Italy's greatest Gothic structures. Its construction took three centuries and involved over 30 architects. It was Pope Urban IV who commissioned it in order to celebrate the Miracle of Bolsena, an event during which a priest found that the sacramental bread was bleeding onto the altar cloth, nowadays kept in the Chapel of the Corporal. A marble band in black and white as well as the colorful façade with columns, spires and sculptures gives the Cathedral a distinct visual impact. Sienese architect Lorenzo Maitani was involved in its most crucial design stages. Inside, head to the Capella di San Brizio to see Luca Signorelli's fresco cycle The Last Judgment, a masterpiece which is said to have inspired Michelangelo's work in the Sistine Chapel.

Other artists who have worked on the Chapel include Fra Angelico and Perugino. The Cathedral is open from 07:30 to 19:15 (with a break between 12:45 and 14:30) in the summer; closes 2 hours earlier in the wintertime.

Lake Trasimeno

Surrounded by hills with sunflowers, the Trasimeno Lake (Lago Trasimeno) is positioned in the northwestern corner of Umbria. Usually crowded in the peak of the summer, the lake is popular with campers and offers a location suitable for watersports and plenty of options for walking and biking. A ferry service connects the waterfront towns in the summer, while the off-season seems to give a somewhat deserted feel to the area, particularly on overcast days.

The lake itself is quite shallow and marshy and is the biggest inland body of water in mainland Italy (128km^2).

Castiglione del Lago

On the southwest corner of the Trasimeno, Castiglione del Lago is the prime spot for those looking for water sports and recreation, with most operators offering such activities based here. It used to be an island in the lake but the gap has been filled in over a period of time. Castiglione has a well preserved historical center and most notable is the Fortress of the Lion (Castello del Leone), a 1247-completed castle. Also check out the Renaissance Town Hall (Palazzo del Comune), today hosting a gallery and a museum.

Panicale

On the south of the Lake, Panicale is like an enormous castle, positioned on a hill overlooking the lake. Of special interest here is the San Sebastiano church where Perugino's 1505 Martyrdom of St. Sebastian can be found, featuring a landscape of the lake. Very recently, another fresco has been uncovered in the church (Madonna in Trono con Angeli Musicanti) which is likely done by Raphael.

Isla Polvese

Although Trasimeno's largest island, the Isola Polvese's only inhabited building is a hostel (Fattoria Il Poggio). Remains of a medieval 14th century castle, a monastery and a church can also be found on it. The island is frequented by school groups studying biodiversity which is being showcased in the Polvese's Garden of Aquatic Plants.

Isla Maggiore

Trasimeno's main inhabited island is Isla Maggiore, a rectangular island with only about 35 inhabitants. It is claimed to have been a favorite of St. Francis who lived here from 1211. The Saint Michael the Archangel church, sitting on a hill, is known as the home of a Crucifixion done by Caporali.

Vernazzano

Vernazzano is a very small village on the north of Trasimeno but is mostly known for its leaning tower. Leaning even more than the tower of Pisa, it was built in 1089 as a section of a castle. Though the castle was severely damaged in the 15th and again in the 17th century, the tower still stands, leaning due to the erosion of its foundations and propped up by steel wires.

Tuoro

Tuoro is mostly known as the location of the Battle of Trasimeno and includes an archeological walking and driving tour of the battlegrounds with description of the famous battle. In 217 BC, in what is known to be one of the most disastrous losses in their history, the Romans were ambushed here by Hannibal and some 16,000 of them were killed as they had to retreat into the lake.

Recommendations for the Budget Traveller

Places To Stay

Hotel Sacro Cuore

Strada del Brozzo 12, 06126 Perugia
Tel: +39 075 33 141
http://www.hotelsacrocuore.com/

Located some 4 kilometers outside the historic center in Perugia, the two-star Sacro Cuore is beautifully positioned on a hilltop and provides views of the Subasio Mountain and Assisi. Two buildings can be found in the hotel complex - one of which used to belong to local nobility - but all rooms are classically decorated and feature TV.

A continental breakfast is also offered each morning and the restaurant on the premises specializes in Umbrian cuisine.

Buses stop 300 meters away and connect the hotel to central Perugia and Assisi. Prices for a double room at the Sacro Cuore start at €50 per night in the early fall season (September), including breakfast.

P&P Assisi Camere

Via Fosse Ardeatine 26/B, 06083 Bastia Umbra
Tel: +39 075 801 2206
http://www.assisicamere.com/

If you want to base yourself around Assisi but prefer the nature to the hoards of tourists, look no further than the P&P Assisi Camere, a bed & breakfast with 6 rooms. Just 4.5 kilometers from Assisi and very close to the Bastia train station, this pension is ideally located in the countryside and offers spacious rooms and free on-site parking. A nice garden also surrounds the complex.

Rates for double rooms at the Assisi Camere start at €50 per night during September, breakfast included.

Hotel Roma

Piazza Santa Chiara, 13/15, 06081 Assisi
Tel: + 39 075 812 390
http://www.assisihotelroma.com/

If you prefer being based in the heart of Assisi, the 3-star Hotel Roma may be a good fit for you with its location right next to the Santa Chiara Basilica and only a 10 minute walk away from the historic center. Its 28 rooms are simple but feature TV and free Wi-Fi. A restaurant can be found nearby, offering Umbrian cuisine.

Prices for a double room and breakfast at the Roma start at €66 per night in September.

Agriturismo Casale dei Frontini

Via Valle Andrea 12 – Frontignano, 06059 Todi
Tel: +39 075 8852174
http://www.casaledeifrontini.it/

Any visit to Umbria would be incomplete without a stay in a local farmhouse (Agriturismo). Sprinkled around the countryside, very affordable and authentic farmhouses are a good choice for budget travelers. One such gem is the Agroturismo Casale dei Frontini just 8 kilometers outside Todi, a former convent surrounded by 20 hectares of land and built some 300 years ago.

Five double bedrooms are included on the premises, all with rustic furnishings and equipped with bathroom, TV and Wi-Fi. Also available are 3 apartments suitable for families. The Casale dei Frontini has a restaurant and both breakfast and half-board options are offered. Prices for a double bedroom and breakfast start at €70 per night.

Hotel Trasimeno

Viale Roma 16A, 06065 Passignano sul Trasimeno
Tel: +39 075 829 355
http://www.hoteltrasimeno.it/home.html

For a budget stay by Trasimeno Lake, check out the Trasimeno Hotel in Passignano sul Trasimeno just a stone throw from the lakeshore. This 3-star family-run hotel features 30 rooms with balconies, all equipped with free Wi-Fi. For bike-lovers who want to explore the lakeside, free rental of bicycles is available from the hotel management.

Double rooms at the Hotel Trasimeno start at about €60 per night during September.

Places To Eat & Drink

Ristorante Pizzeria Capri

Corso Cavour 28, Perugia
Tel: + 39 075 573 1880
http://www.capripizzeria.it/

For delicious pizzas, try the Capri Pizzeria in a tiny street in central Perugia. The atmosphere here is relaxed and friendly and the place gets packed with locals quickly without sacrificing on the quality of service. During the summer, outdoor seating is preferred. The pizzas are cooked in a traditional wood oven and include traditional Umbrian ingredients. Save some room for the panacotta as well. Prices around €10 per pizza.

Osteria Piazzetta dell'Erba

Via San Gabriele dell'Addolorata 15/A, 06081 Assisi
Tel: + 39 075 815 352

Locals flock to this restaurant in Assisi, an understandable phenomenon given the delightful menu. Appetizers are sophisticated, pasta dishes are varied (try the lasagna) and the deserts are truly tasty, especially the homemade biscuits. The wines are local and reasonably priced. Expect the bill to start at around €30 per person, including wine.

Osteria del Trivio

Via del Trivio, 16, Spoleto
Tel: +39 074 344 349

In Spoleto, check out the Osteria del Trivio right off the main street in the upper town. The décor in this family run Osteria is truly Umbrian and the food is delightful, particularly the antipasto. Rely on the waiter's suggestions about what is particularly fresh and recommended and do try the house wine. The average price per person for a first and second course, dessert, wine and coffee starts at €30.

Il Giglio d'Oro

Piazza Duomo, 8, 05018 Orvieto
Tel: +39 076 334 1903
http://www.ilgigliodoro.it/

In Orveto and close to the Cathedral, splurge at the Il Giglio d'Oro which looks out onto the Duomo. The service is very attentive and professional and some menu highlights include the eggplant souffle, the pasta with black truffles and the zuccotto de ricotta dessert. Don't skip the complimentary amuse bouche with the honey topped ricotta. A very filling three course dinner with wine for two starts at around €60 at this prime location in Orvieto.

DivinPeccato

Trasimeno 95, Panicarola, 06060 Castiglione del Lago
Tel: +39 075 968 0118
http://www.ristorantedivinpeccato.com/

When in Castiglione del Lago, head to the DivinPeccato just 10 kilometers away in Panicarola. The chef in the DivinPeccato is local and the staff is friendly and warm. An extensive wine list as well as a mixed array of traditional and modern dishes is offered. A fixed price seasonal menu is reasonably priced (€30) and includes appetizer, first and second course, dessert, water, wine and coffee in this excellent tucked away restaurant.

Places To Shop

Mercato Mensile Antiquariato

Perugia

If your visit to Perugia happens to be on the fourth weekend of the month, the Mercato Mensile Antiquariato (an antiquities market) may be a good way to spend some time around Piazza Italia and Giardine Carducci. Frames, furniture, stamps, postcards and old prints are all on sale here from 09:00 to 19:00.

Augusta Perusia Cioccolate e Gelateria

Via Pinturicchio 2, Perugia
Tel: +39 075 573 4577
www.cioccolatoaugustaperusia.it

Perugia is chocoholics' heaven and the Augusta Perusia Cioccolate e Gelateria is not to be missed for a heavy dose of delightful treats. Opened since 2000 and owned by Giordano, one of its most famous items are traditional baci (kisses – chocolate covered hazelnuts) which are made by the original recipe and are a great food gift from Perugia.

Leo Grilli Arte

Via dei Consoli 78, Gubbio

Ceremic lovers visiting Gubbio should definitely check out the Leo Grilli Arte workshop located in a 15th century mansion. Gubbio has a longstanding tradition in ceramics and maestro Leo still pops into the workshop daily even though he has passed on the management to his daughter. Crammed floor to ceiling with ceramics in various styles, this is true heaven for those who appreciate the artform.

Terra Umbra

Via San Paolo 12/A, 06081 Assisi
Tel: +39 075 815 5350

For hand-embroidered linens and other antique items such as ceramics, glass, baskets and candles, visit the Terra Umbra store in Assisi. The store also sells organic Umbria foodstuffs including wine, olive oil and honey as well as natural cosmetics made from white clay, almond and seaweed.

Bartolomei Orvieto

Corso Cavour 97, 05018 Orvieto
Tel: +39 076 334 4540
http://www.oleificiobartolomei.it/it/index.php

If you are interested in food souvenirs, a visit to the Bartolomei shop in Orvieto is a good idea. The shop sells a wide range of local products, most notably olive oil but also olive paste, wine and truffles. The owners will be happy to provide a sampling of the oil and wine in the true Italian tradition.

CPSIA information can be obtained
at www.ICGtesting.com
Printed in the USA
BVHW031306060822
643972BV00018B/173